STORIES OF THE PROPHETS

The Story of Muhammad ﷺ

IN MADINAH

Summarised and Illustrated

by Abu Zahir

"O! you Arabs, here comes the Prophet you have all been waiting for," shouted a man from the tribe of Bani Israel.

There appeared two shapes in the distance, coming through the hot desert haze towards Madinah.

When they heard the shout, every man, woman and child dropped whatever

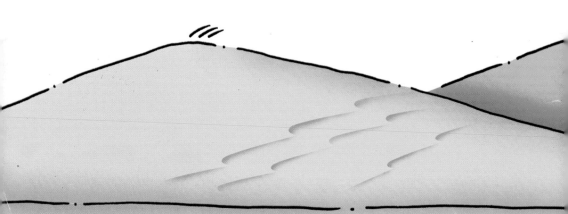

they were doing and lined the streets of Madinah.

Many of the new Muslims in Madinah had not met the Messenger, Muhammad ﷺ . At first they mistook Abu Bakr ؓ for Muhammad ﷺ, until he covered Muhammad ﷺ with his own cloth from the blazing, afternoon sun.

Muhammad ﷺ stayed a few days in a place called Quba and built the first Masjid there. He then rode his camel towards the centre of Madinah and let Allah ﷻ guide his camel until she came to rest on her knees.

The land on which the camel came to rest belonged to two orphans called Suhail and Sahl. It is here that Muhammad ﷺ built his Masjid and his home next to it. The Muslims who welcomed Muhammad ﷺ and the Muhaajirun were called the Ansar or the helpers.

Muhammad ﷺ soon became the leader of Madinah. The Muhaajirun and the Ansar were true brothers in Islam.

The Ansar loved Muhammad ﷺ and the Muhaajirun that they were willing to share their wealth, property and even their wives.

The other tribes who were mainly Jews were given protection under the Muslims and were allowed to live in peace.

After the Messenger Muhammad ﷺ came to Madinah, more people became Muslims and those who went to Abyssinia, came back later to join them.

Meanwhile the Quraish who were angry with Muhammad ﷺ for leaving Makkah, were preparing an army to fight the Muslims in Madinah.

An army of about thousand men were marching to Madinah under Abu Jahl, the leader of the Quraish.

This was the first time that Allah ﷻ gave the Muslims the right to fight and defend Islam.

Many Muslims were now ready to sacrifice their lives for Allah ﷻ.

Muhammad ﷺ put all his trust in Allah ﷻ, to give the Muslims victory over their enemies.

When the battle of Badr began, the Muslims fought bravely and killed many of the Quraish leaders including Abu Jahl.

There were three hundred Muslims against a thousand Quraish. Allah ﷻ the Most Merciful sent down the angels to fight alongside the Muslim army.

Victory was for the Muslims on that day and the Quraish army ran away in fear.

Muhammad ﷺ ordered the Muslims to be kind to their prisoners and to share the war booty among the Muslims.

The Muslims grew strong in their belief and in their support for Muhammad ﷺ after this victory. Now the tribes around Madinah were afraid of the brave Muslim Army.

The next battle between the Quraish and the Muslims was fought on a mountain called Uhud, four kilometres north of Madinah.

The Quraish were angry at their loss to the Muslims at Badr. This time they were better prepared, with an army of three thousand men, two hundred on horses and seven hundred wearing armour plates. The Muslim army could only gather a thousand men, of which there were only a hundred who wore armour plates.

Muhammad ﷺ was keen to fight the enemies of Islam in Madinah but the young Muhaajirun and the Ansar were keen to fight them at Mount Uhud.

When Muhammad ﷺ and his army reached Mount Uhud, the leader of the hypocrites, Abdullah bin Ubay, along with three hundred men ran back to Madinah.

They were afraid when they saw the huge Quraish army coming towards them.

Muhammad ﷺ was now left with only seven hundred men. The battle began soon after the morning Fajr prayer.

Fifty archers with Abdullah bin Jubayr, as their leader, were on top of Mount Uhud.

The archers were ordered not to leave their positions in victory or defeat.

The Muslim army was lined up, facing the enemy with their backs to the mountain.

When the enemy charged, the archers rained their arrows on them. Many of the Quraish were killed.

When the Muslims started winning, the Quraish turned their backs and started to run away.

Some of the archers got so excited when they saw the enemy retreating that they came down the mountain to collect their booty.

They left behind their leader, Abdullah bin Jubayr thus disobeying the orders of Muhammad ﷺ.

All of a sudden, the arrows stopped coming. The Quraish saw this and circled the mountain, starting an attack from behind Mount Uhud.

By now there were very few archers to protect the Muslim army and they were in big trouble!

The Muslim army after having tasted victory were now losing men.

Muhammad ﷺ was badly injured when a stone struck his face and he lost his front tooth. There were many fearless companions who defended Muhammad ﷺ bravely.

One of them was Abu Dujaanah, who used his body as a shield, protecting the Messenger from the arrows.

Allah ﷻ taught the
Muslims a lesson by taking
away their victory, for
disobeying the orders of His
Messenger Muhammad ﷺ.
This was indeed a test for
those Muslims who fought at the
battle of Mount Uhud.

Of the Muslims, seventy men were killed, amongst whom was Muhammad's brave uncle, Hamzah ﷺ .

Many attempts were made on the life of Muhammad ﷺ Finally the Quraish who were now exhausted from the battle returned to Makkah.

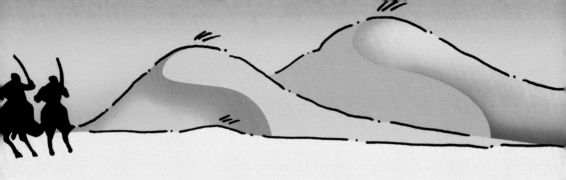

After the battle of Uhud, the Muslims buried their dead. They then praised and thanked Allah ﷻ the Most Gracious and the Most Merciful. Many of those who died bravely in the battle were promised Paradise.

The rest of the Muslim army along with Muhammad ﷺ returned to Madinah safely.

In Madinah, the neighbouring tribes and the Jews gave Muhammad ﷺ and the Muslims endless problems.

Allah ﷻ the All-Mighty helped the Muslims overcome the plots of their enemies.

Some of the Jews who were expelled from Madinah joined the Quraish.

This time they came with an army of ten thousand men, with Abu Sufyan as their leader.

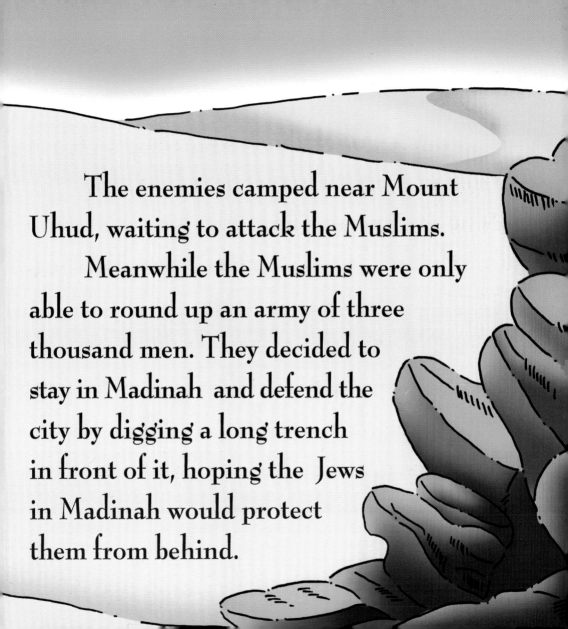

The enemies camped near Mount Uhud, waiting to attack the Muslims. Meanwhile the Muslims were only able to round up an army of three thousand men. They decided to stay in Madinah and defend the city by digging a long trench in front of it, hoping the Jews in Madinah would protect them from behind.

At the battle of Al-Ahzaab, the trenches were the biggest surprise for the enemies. They attacked the city of Madinah for twenty days, but the Muslims fought the enemies off bravely.

The army of the Quraish was soon disunited and their leaders were fighting.

amongst themselves. One night, Allah ﷻ sent a violent sand storm which blew their tents away and scattered their horses.

That same night Abu Sufyan and his army fled to Makkah, but some of them asked the Jews in Madinah for help. The Jews who were under the protection of the Muslims, disobeyed Muhammad ﷺ by helping them. This made the Muslims very angry with the Jews.

Just as the Muslim army was putting their weapons away, Allah ﷻ sent the angel Jibreel عليه السلام to remind Muhammad ﷺ to go after the tribe of Banu Qurayzah, the Jewish tribe which secretly helped the Quraish during the battle of Al-Ahzaab. The Muslim army then marched towards the

fortress of Banu Qurayzah and attacked them for twenty-five days until they surrendered. All their warriors were killed and their booty was shared amongst the Muslims.

After all the Jews were driven out of Madinah, the Muslims finally enjoyed some peace.

One day, Muhammad ﷺ had a dream where the Muslims were performing Umrah, with their heads being shaved.

Muhammad ﷺ told his companions to make preparations to visit Makkah.

Many of the Muslims were excited and eager for this visit, because it had been six years since they had all left Makkah. One thousand five hundred Muslims made the

journey to Makkah along with Muhammad ﷺ. None took their weapons with them.

In the meantime, the Quraish were preparing an army to stop the Muslims from visiting the Ka'bah.

When the Muslims reached the border of Makkah, Muhammad ﷺ sent a few of his closest companions to meet the leaders of the Quraish.

The companions were not welcomed by the Quraish leaders as they were angry with the Muslims for their losses in the battle of Al-Ahzaab.

After much difficulty a treaty was made between the leaders of the Quraish and Muhammad ﷺ. This treaty was called the treaty of Al-Hudaibiyah.

The Quraish and the Muslims made a promise that they would not fight each other

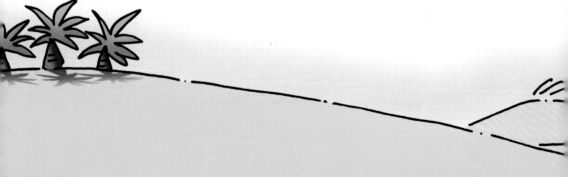

for ten years. The Muslims had to return to Madinah without visiting the Ka'bah. They could only return to Makkah the following year for three days, to perform Umrah, the lesser pilgrimage.

The Muslims were disappointed but they all obeyed Muhammad ﷺ by shaving their heads and making their sacrifice in the name of Allah ﷻ. They went back to Madinah, longing to come back the next year.

After Muhammad ﷺ returned from Hudaibiyah, he asked a few of his able companions to take the Message of Islam to the lands beyond Arabia. These lands were ruled by Kings and Emperors.

The King of Persia, Chosroes, did not welcome the companions kindly. When Muhammad ﷺ heard the news, he said that Islam would spread beyond the Persian Empire.

The companions who visited Heraclius, the Emperor of Rome, were warmly welcomed.

He treated them with respect and sent back a reply along with some gifts.

Heraclius refused to accept Islam even though he knew that Muhammad ﷺ was the true Messenger of Allah ﷻ.

Another group was sent with the message of Islam to the King of Damascus.

This King was so furious that he said, "Who ever dares to rid me of my country, I will fight him." He arrogantly rejected the tion to Islam.

One year had gone by and it was time for the Muslims to go for Umrah.

Muhammad ﷺ and two thousand Muslims along with their camels for sacrifice made the journey to Makkah.

This time they entered Makkah without any problems. Many of the Quraish were hiding in the mountains and watching the Muslims.

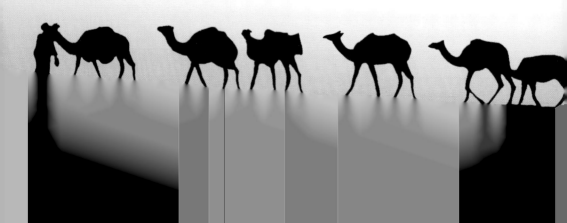

The Muslims were busy following their leader Muhammad ﷺ.

They did the Tawaf by going round the Ka'bah seven times. Then they walked and ran between the two hills of Safa and Marwa, seven times.

Finally they made their sacrifice and shaved their heads, seeking the mercy and forgiveness of Allah ﷻ, the Most Merciful.

They were able to complete their Umrah for the first time in many years.

After three days in Makkah, the Messenger, Muhammad ﷺ together with the Muslims left for Madinah.

They kept their promise to the Quraish which they made a year ago.

Soon after the Muslims returned to Madinah, Khalid bin Walid 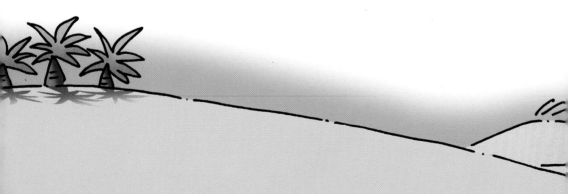, one of the bravest fighters amongst the Quraish, accepted Islam. He led the Muslims to many victories over the enemies of Islam. He was known as the "Sword of Allah ﷻ."

The Quraish were the first to break the promise of Al-Hudaibiyah by fighting those who were under the protection of the Muslims in Madinah.

Muhammad 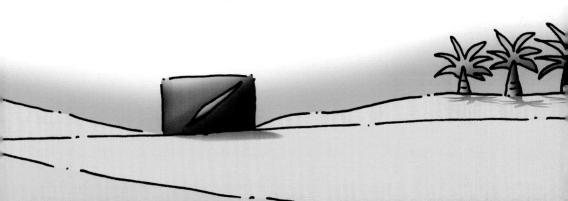 decided it was time to end all fighting with the Quraish.

He ﷺ ordered an army of ten thousand men to march towards Mecca. They marched for eight days until they reached a place called Marr Az-Zahran which is on the border of Mecca.

The Quraish were not ready for a battle so they sent Abu Sufyaan, a leader of the Quraish, to meet Muhammad ﷺ. He asked the Muslims to return to Madinah in peace.

At this meeting Abu Sufyaan accepted Islam. He then went back to Mecca with a message from Muhammad ﷺ to give up fighting and to make way for the Muslim army to take over Mecca.

Abu Sufyaan said to the Quraish, "He who seeks protection in my house is safe, whoever stays in their houses are safe and those who lived around the Ka'bah are safe too."

Having announced that to the people of Quraish, he waited for the Muslim army to arrive.

When the army entered Makkah with Muhammad ﷺ on his favourite camel, Qaswa, the streets were deserted and there were hardly anyone, willing to fight them.

Allah ﷻ the All Mighty gave the Muslims victory over those who wished to defeat His Messenger, Muhammad ﷺ .

Muhammad ﷺ asked the Muslims to be kind to the Quraish. He ordered the Muslim army to break all the idols that were around the Ka'bah. Having completed the task, he spoke to all the Muslims who were in Makkah.

He said that Allah ﷻ has created us from a male and female and made us into nations and tribes that we may know one another. Verily, the best among you is the one who fears Allah ﷻ and does good, for He knows and sees everything that is happening around us."

The Muslims were now the guardians of Makkah. By the mercy of Muhammad ﷺ and his companions, the worst enemies of the Muslims were forgiven. They, in turn accepted Islam. The whole of Arabia was now under the Muslims.

Muhammad ﷺ sent small groups of trusted companions to invite their neighbours to Islam.

They were warned to have fear of Allah ﷻ in their mission and to break the idols of Uzza, Suwwa and Manat.

One of the tribes that put up a fight were the Arabs of Taaif. The Muslim army surrounded the city until they surrendered.

When they were taken as prisoners, they were treated kindly by Muhammad ﷺ and set free. Soon they too became Muslims.

Many of the tribes heard about Islam and the kindness shown by the Muslims to the Quraish in Makkah.

They sent their leaders to meet Muhammad ﷺ. Having met him, they had no doubt that he was indeed a true Messenger of Allah ﷻ.

They accepted Islam and went home to teach their own tribes to worship Allah ﷻ Alone. They broke all the idols that they had used to worship in the past, until there was none left in all of Arabia.

Muhammad ﷺ and his companions returned to Madinah soon after all the people had accepted Islam in Makkah.

After having successfully completed his mission of calling the people to Islam, he knew that his days in this life were numbered.

Muhammad ﷺ called all his people to perform the Hajj pilgrimage. Thousands of Muslims from around Arabia joined him.

They came by land and from over the mountains, with some walking while others came riding.

They first performed Umrah before the Hajj. They all followed Muhammad ﷺ in all his acts of worship. They stayed in Mina before going to Mount Arafat. There, the Messenger of Allah ﷺ spoke to all the Muslims

who had gathered on the mountain. He told his people to listen carefully to what he had to say for he may not be amongst them after that year.

Muhammad ﷺ wanted the Muslims to support each other and to be kind to their families and slaves. He reminded them that every Muslim was a brother to one another and should do good and stop all evil.

He said," Tell your brothers who are not here today, for they may remember what they heard better than the one who heard it ."

He reminded them to fear Allah ﷻ and obey Him, the All Mighty. There were many Muslims who had tears in their eyes while listening to him.

After finally throwing seven pebbles at the Jamrah, they sacrificed their camels and then haved their heads.

The Muslims finished their Hajj by doing a farewell Tawaf round the Ka'bah. and then they all returned home.

Before Muhammad ﷺ became ill, he sent a huge army from Madinah to spread Islam under the leadership of Usaamah bin Zaid who was only twenty years of age.

The message of Islam spread from Arabia to Spain and from Indonesia to far off China.

Just as the Muslim army had left Madinah, Muhammad ﷺ was overcome by his illness.

He spent his last days leading his followers in prayer. When his illness became worse he got the permission of his wives to spend the last few days of his life with his youngest wife, Ayesha ﵂.

Muhammad ﷺ was in a lot of pain and often passed out while lying on the lap of Ayesha رضي الله عنها.

Whenever he woke up from his illness, he would ask Ayesha رضي الله عنها repeatedly if the people had prayed.

This shows the importance of prayer, which is to worship Allah سبحانه وتعالى Alone without joining partners to Him.

Death came to him on a Monday , as Muhammad ﷺ was resting in the arms of Ayesha رضي الله عنها .

His greatest miracle was the Quran, the words of Allah سبحانه وتعالى, that was sent to guide all of mankind through the angel Jibreel عليه السلام.

Those who obey Allah سبحانه وتعالى will be rewarded with Paradise.

In Paradise we can meet Muhammad ﷺ and all the